PROFESSOR RAMAN PRINJA

The FUTURE of the UNIVERSE

THE NEXT TRILLION YEARS AND BEYOND

ILLUSTRATED BY **JAN BIELECKI**

WAYLAND

ROYAL OBSERVATORY GREENWICH

To Kamini, Vikas and Sachin – R. P.
For Inessa – J. B.

First published in Great Britain in 2022 by Wayland
Text © Raman Prinja, 2022
Design and Illustration © Hodder and Stoughton, 2022

Commissioning Editor: Grace Glendinning
Designers: Claire Jones and Kate Wiliwinska
Illustrations: Jan Bielecki

ISBN: 978 1 5263 1646 2 HBK
ISBN: 978 1 5263 1647 9 PBK
ISBN: 978 1 5263 2225 8 EBOOK

FSC
www.fsc.org
MIX
Paper from
responsible sources
FSC® C114687

Printed and bound in China

Wayland, an imprint of
Hachette Children's Group
Part of Hodder and Stoughton

Carmelite House
50 Victoria Embankment
London EC4Y 0DZ

An Hachette UK Company
www.hachette.co.uk
www.hachettechildrens.co.uk

CONTENTS

FOREWORD

Looking up at the night sky, the Universe might look like a tranquil, unchanging place. Its vastness is familiar – the skies look practically the same when you're an adult as they did when you were a young child. The Universe has the feeling of being eternal. But, really, the Universe is constantly changing – we just don't notice it. We can see objects like planets and the Moon gliding across space because they are closest to us, but far beyond our solar system are trillions of stars and galaxies hurtling and expanding across the cosmos. We can't see their movements in our skies because they are enormously far away from our little corner of the Universe.

You may have already read books about the 13.8-billion-year history and formation of the cosmos, but how much do you know about its future? This fascinating book will reveal all. We cannot flip back the pages of the Universe's story to replay its past, and likewise we don't have a time machine to zoom forward into its future. But scientists are able to piece together evidence to have a pretty good idea. By looking at a snapshot of the Universe in the present, scientists can begin to work out the evolutionary paths of objects within it. This knowledge allows scientists to describe changes to come, by applying current astronomical facts to the future behaviour of the Universe. From observations over time, it's clear that the whole Universe is changing – and it will certainly look quite different in billions of years to come.

Not only is space expanding but so too is our understanding and interpretation of the scientific principles that control the fate of the cosmos and everything within it. Space is a place of many mysteries with thousands of scientists across the world working to solve them. Perhaps you could become part of the next generation of scientists and take up the challenge – there will always be more fascinating, unresolved questions to answer. What an inspiring career that would be!

This search for scientific knowledge is for everyone and it is interwoven into our daily lives, whether we realise it or not. By its nature, science evokes curiosity and ingenuity – values that Professor Raman Prinja and we at Royal Observatory Greenwich endeavour to foster in people of all ages. We are proud to support books such as this one, written by a scientist whose passion for this knowledge-hunt is infectious.

Looking to the future naturally enlivens our inquisitiveness and fans the fire of our imagination. We hope that after reading this book you can look up at our Universe and make more sense of that perplexing expanse of space.

Dhara Patel
Senior Manager of Astronomy Education
Royal Observatory Greenwich

ROYAL
OBSERVATORY
GREENWICH

**Midnight on
1 January**

The Big Bang
occurs

February

15 March

Our Milky Way
Galaxy forms (which
actually happened
11 billion years ago)

April

May

June

July

August

September

October

November

COSMIC TIMELINES

Our planet, our solar system, our galaxy and even the entire Universe change as time goes by. Planets are gliding in orbits around the Sun, new comets pass through our skies, old stars die, new stars are born, and hundreds of billions of galaxies are racing away from each other in space. In this book we are going to take a very special journey to explore the future timeline of changes to the Universe.

We often use timelines to take us back through the Earth's past. In human history we have timelines that go back thousands of years to describe life in various points of history: prehistoric times, ancient Roman civilisations, Chinese dynasties, the Industrial Revolution – right up to the 21st century.

Our universe also has a past timeline, but it stretches back **13.8 billion** years! That's when the Universe is thought to have begun with a Big Bang. Matter, energy, space and time all came into existence at this moment. During this 13.8-billion-year history, the amazing Universe formed atoms, stars, galaxies and eventually planets, including our Earth, where life thrives today.

31 August

The solar system
starts to assemble

3 September

Our planet Earth
has formed

30 September

Bacteria made of single
cells appear on Earth

5 December

More complicated
organisms made of many
cells appear on Earth

A (time) scale model

Time periods that cover billions of years can be difficult to grasp because they are so much longer than what we are used to in our everyday lives. So, imagine instead that we compress the entire 13.8-billion-year history of the Universe into a single (Earth) calendar year. On this 1-year scale model, every **month** represents **just over a billion years** and every **hour** is around **1.5 million years!** The image below shows major events of the Universe marked out along the model year.

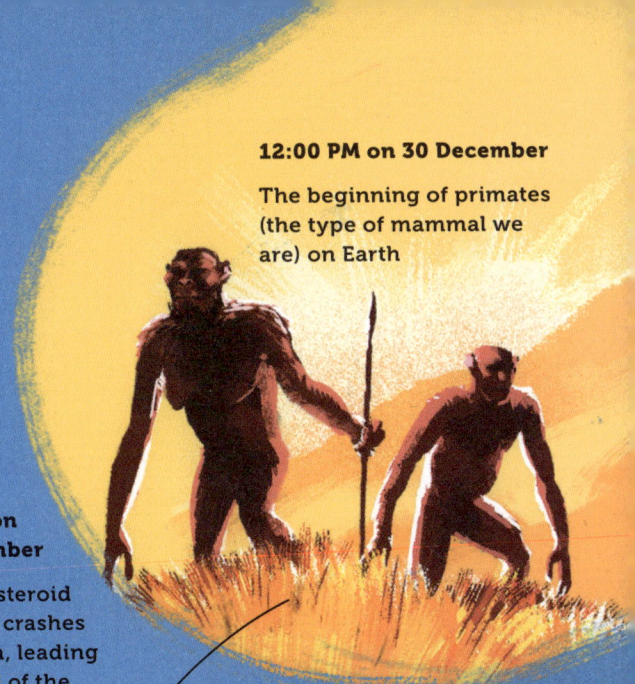

12:00 PM on 30 December

The beginning of primates (the type of mammal we are) on Earth

6:00 AM on 30 December

A giant asteroid or comet crashes into Earth, leading to the end of the dinosaurs' reign

25 December

Dinosaurs are stomping around on our planet

11:59 PM on 31 December

Pyramids built by the ancient Egyptians

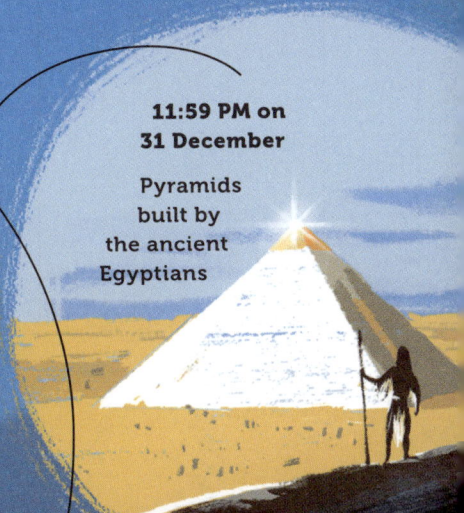

Our model shows that the full span of human history is incredibly tiny when compared to the vast age of the Universe.

December

Final 10 seconds of the year

Entire human history, from ancient Egyptians to today!

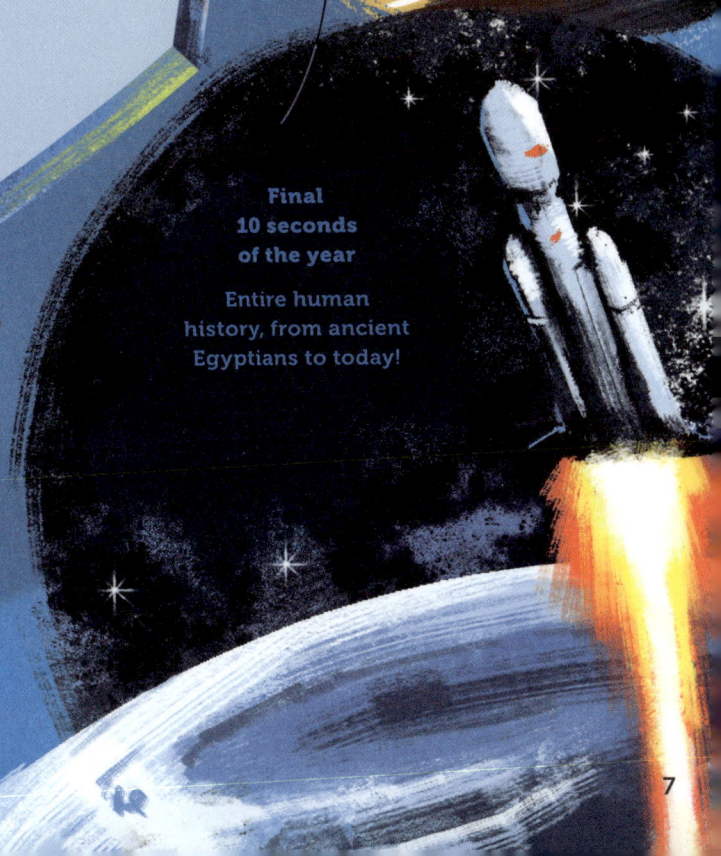

A GREAT JOURNEY INTO THE FUTURE

In the pages to come, instead of looking back, we will look ahead thousands, millions, billions and even trillions of years to explore some amazing events and changes that scientists predict will occur in the Universe. Our voyage into the future will take us to new constellations, exploding stars, new planet rings, an awesome galaxy crash and the movements of swarms of galaxies. Finally, we will look at the dark end of the Universe itself, trillions and trillions of years from now. (A trillion is a huge number written as 1,000,000,000,000!)

The future events of the Universe that we will discover in this book are not guesses. Scientists are able to confidently predict changes to come by using their understanding of how the Universe has *already changed* over the past 13.8 billion years. We have scientific laws that help us to understand how forces, such as gravity, act on objects in space.

Using subjects such as physics, astronomy and mathematics, scientists study the motion of matter in the Universe, and how it behaves with energy and light. Generations of scientists to come (which could include YOU!) will continue to learn and improve upon our understanding of each future wonder.

Let's take our knowledge of the past and current Universe and start a great exploration into its future. With each chapter, we will jump further and further ahead in time, along the Future Clock timeline of the magnificent Universe.

Gravity rules

Gravity is one of the key forces in the Universe. Though gravity is the weakest of all the fundamental forces of nature, it is the most important force in the study of space and astronomy. Every object that has a mass will have a gravitational force that acts on other objects:

- **The gravitational force of the Sun acts on the planets to keep them in orbit and prevents them flying off into interstellar space.**

- **The gravitational force of the Earth holds us firmly on the planet's surface.**

- **It is gravity that holds together the billions of stars that make up our beautiful, spiral-shaped Milky Way Galaxy.**

Gravity has been around since the very beginning of the Universe, and we believe that it works the same way everywhere in the Universe.

RETURN OF THE
GREAT COMETS

Cosmic snowballs

Comets are the icy wanderers of the solar system. They are small objects made up of rock and ice that are left over from the formation of planets and moons about **4.5 billion** years ago. Comets help us to understand the material that was present when planets first formed, since they have remained largely unchanged since that time.

Each comet has a tiny frozen part called a nucleus, which is usually about **1 km to 20 km** in diameter. The nucleus is made of icy lumps, frozen gases and bits of rock and dust. You can think of them as dirty snowballs in space. Some scientists think that comets originally brought some of the water to make Earth's oceans, when they crashed into our planet.

Looping the Sun

Comets spend most of their lives billions or even trillions of kilometres from the Sun. However, they have the strangest orbits in the solar system – they swoop far out beyond all the planets and then they dive in close to the Sun. This is known as an elliptical orbit.

When their egg-shaped orbits bring them close to the Sun, the comets heat up and spew out gas and dust, which then forms a tail that stretches away from the Sun for millions of kilometres. This is what we can see glowing in the sky when comets make their trips past Earth.

Predicting a comet

One of the most famous comets is Comet Halley. It is named after the English astronomer and mathematician Edmond Halley. He carefully studied historical accounts of comets that were seen in the night sky in 1531, 1607 and 1682. At the same time, the English mathematician Sir Isaac Newton was working on his theory of gravity and the laws of motion. Halley used this theory to calculate accurately the orbit of the comet.

This is called a periodic comet and Halley predicted the comet would pass close to the Earth again in 1758. Sadly, Halley died in 1742 and could not view the comet's return with his own eyes. However, other astronomers were able to see it and prove that Halley's prediction was correct! Comet Halley is on a regular (or periodic) orbit around the Sun, and each lap takes 75–76 years to complete.

The nucleus of Comet Halley is one of the darkest objects in the solar system since it reflects back very little of the sunlight that falls on it.

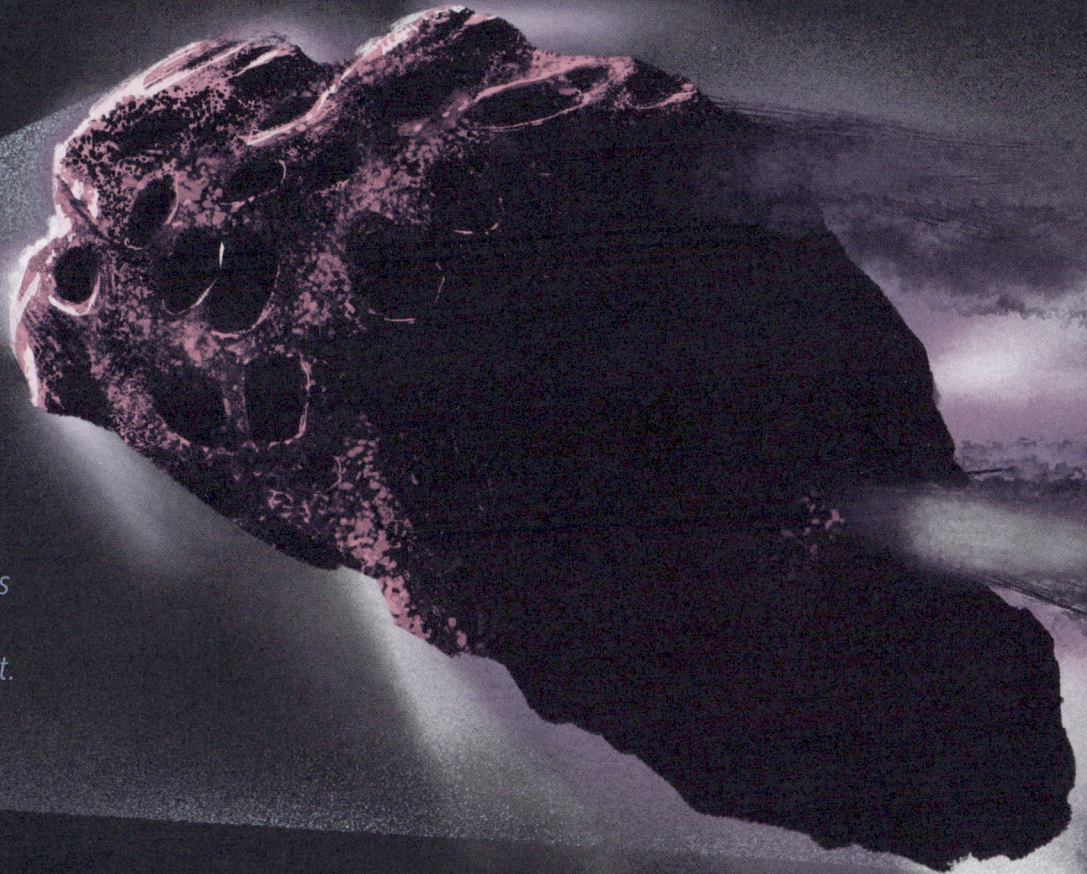

At a particular point on each lap, Comet Halley glides past the Earth. Its appearance in 1910 was spectacular, as it flew by only 22 million km from the Earth (this is actually really close for a comet!).

When Comet Halley last came near to the Earth in 1986, it was the first time we could use spacecraft to get really close to study it. The European Space Agency (ESA) sent the Giotto spacecraft to meet the comet and it beamed back some spectacular images of the nucleus, which is 15 km by 8 km in size.

The next great show

Now we move into the future. Using the laws of gravity, scientists can predict very accurately that Comet Halley will return to our skies in 2061, on its regular journey around the Sun.

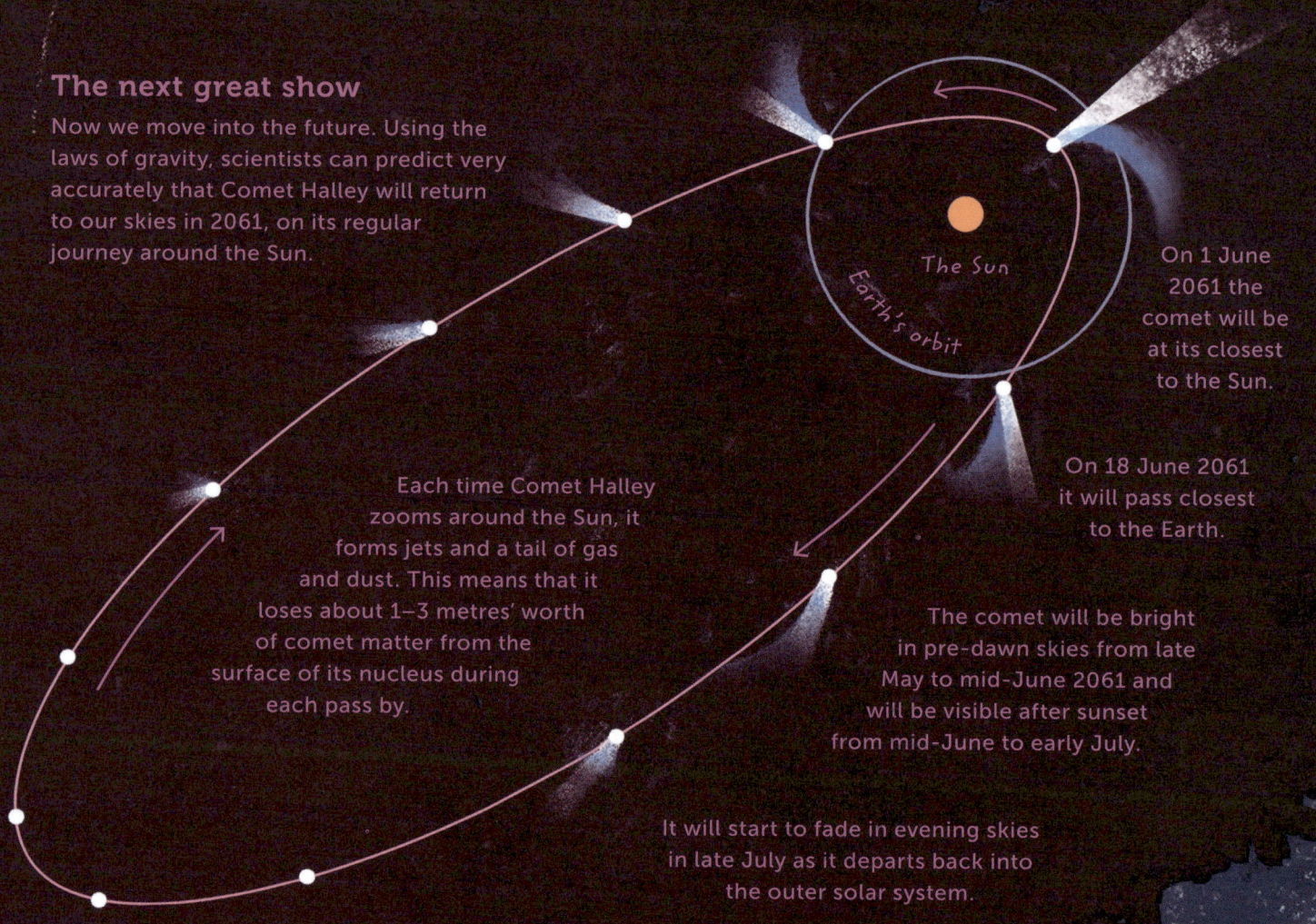

The Sun

Earth's orbit

Each time Comet Halley zooms around the Sun, it forms jets and a tail of gas and dust. This means that it loses about 1–3 metres' worth of comet matter from the surface of its nucleus during each pass by.

On 1 June 2061 the comet will be at its closest to the Sun.

On 18 June 2061 it will pass closest to the Earth.

The comet will be bright in pre-dawn skies from late May to mid-June 2061 and will be visible after sunset from mid-June to early July.

It will start to fade in evening skies in late July as it departs back into the outer solar system.

Some scientists predict that Comet Halley may manage about 300 more trips around the Sun before it breaks up into pieces. That means it should still grace our skies for up to around 23,000 more years.

More comets coming

Comet Hale-Bopp is another great periodic comet. It was a spectacular sight we could see with just our eyes for many months in 1997. Astronomers have worked out that it has a periodic orbit that is much longer than that of Comet Halley. Hale-Bopp takes more than 2,000 years to complete just one lap around the Sun. It is predicted to make its next great show in our skies in the year 4385!

EARTH'S WOBBLE

Wheels, merry-go-rounds and planets all spin around an axis. The Earth's axis is an imaginary line that runs from the North to South poles, directly passing through the planet's centre. Though we can't feel it, the Earth's surface is rotating around this axis at more than 1,000 km per hour. This gives us our day and night cycle every 24 hours. Thankfully, turning at this dizzying speed, we aren't flung off the planet because the downward force of Earth's gravity holds us firmly to the ground.

Tilted Earth

Scientists think that billions of years ago, when the Earth was very young, a large object hit the planet and knocked it so that its axis now leans over a bit. The axis of the Earth is tilted by an angle of 23.4 degrees.

This particular tilt, as we experience it today, is part of the reason the Earth is a varied, balanced place supporting human life! Our seasons happen because of this tilt. Throughout the year, when the North Pole is angled towards the Sun, it is summer in the northern hemisphere. It feels hotter then because the Sun's rays shine through Earth's atmosphere in a nearly straight line instead of an angle. This means the light does not spread out as much, so there's more energy hitting any given spot on the surface. About 6 months later, when the South Pole is angled towards the Sun, it is winter in the northern hemisphere and summer in the southern hemisphere.

Vega

Polaris

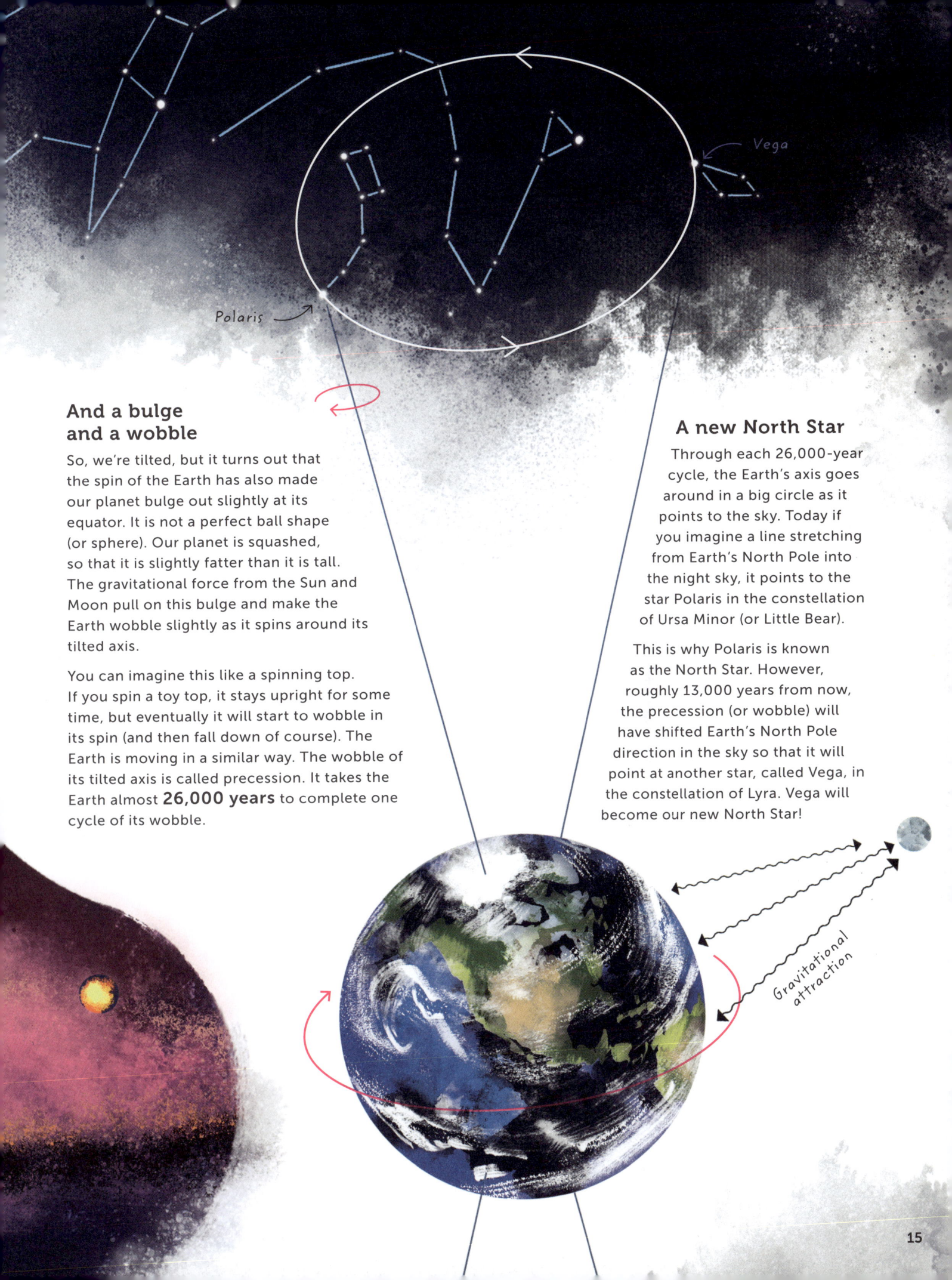

And a bulge and a wobble

So, we're tilted, but it turns out that the spin of the Earth has also made our planet bulge out slightly at its equator. It is not a perfect ball shape (or sphere). Our planet is squashed, so that it is slightly fatter than it is tall. The gravitational force from the Sun and Moon pull on this bulge and make the Earth wobble slightly as it spins around its tilted axis.

You can imagine this like a spinning top. If you spin a toy top, it stays upright for some time, but eventually it will start to wobble in its spin (and then fall down of course). The Earth is moving in a similar way. The wobble of its tilted axis is called precession. It takes the Earth almost **26,000 years** to complete one cycle of its wobble.

A new North Star

Through each 26,000-year cycle, the Earth's axis goes around in a big circle as it points to the sky. Today if you imagine a line stretching from Earth's North Pole into the night sky, it points to the star Polaris in the constellation of Ursa Minor (or Little Bear).

This is why Polaris is known as the North Star. However, roughly 13,000 years from now, the precession (or wobble) will have shifted Earth's North Pole direction in the sky so that it will point at another star, called Vega, in the constellation of Lyra. Vega will become our new North Star!

Gravitational attraction

Hotter summers and cooler winters

With this shift 13,000 years from now, the Earth will still have its seasons in the same months of the calendar each year, but the precession of Earth's axis will have changed **where in our orbit** the seasons happen. In about 13,000 years, the Earth's axis will have wobbled enough so that summer in the northern hemisphere will happen when the Earth is slightly closer to the Sun on its egg-shaped orbital path.

We are currently closest to the Sun in January, but in 13,000 years we will be closest to the Sun in July.

CALENDAR OF SEASONS

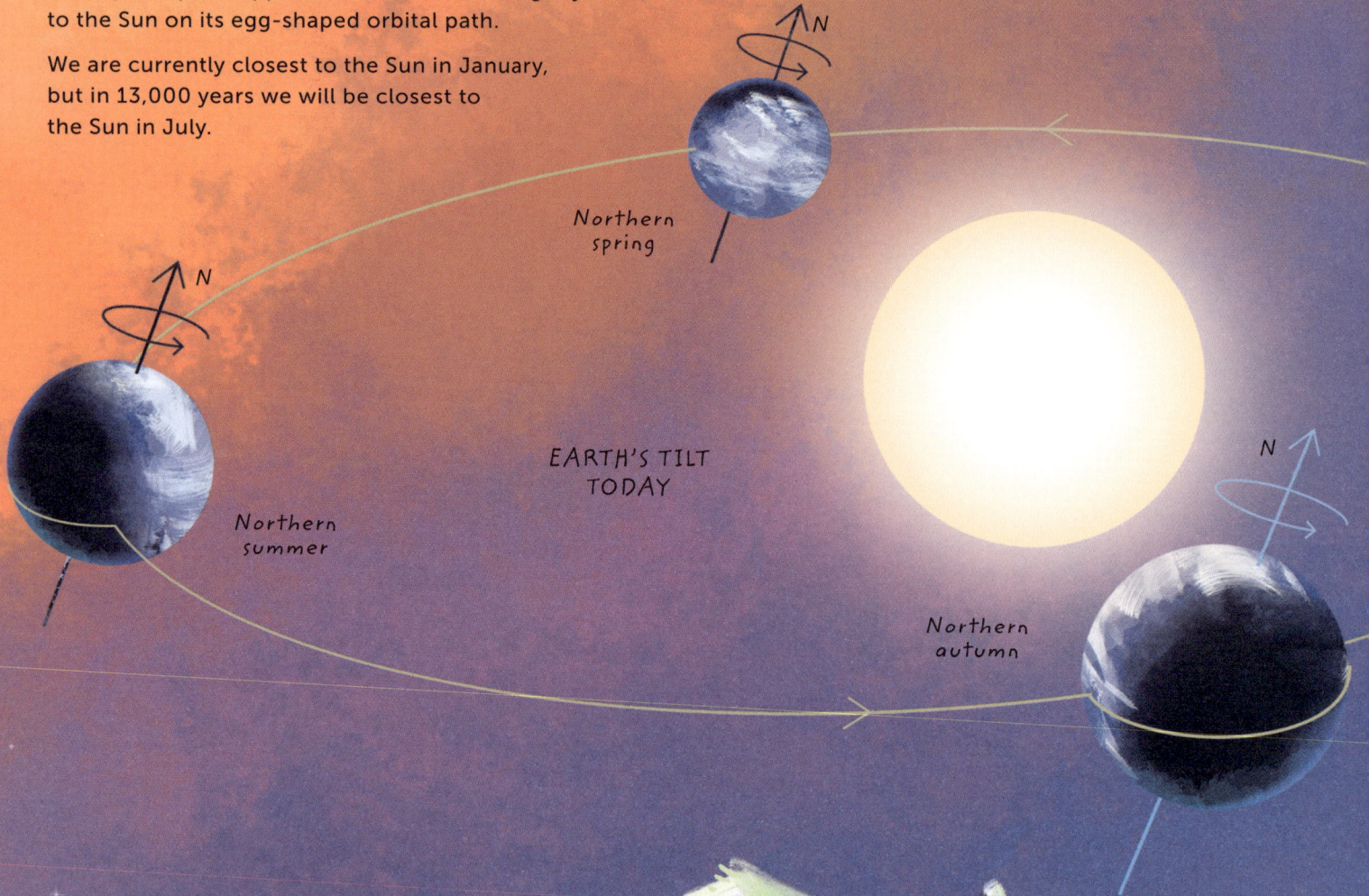

N

Northern spring

N

Northern summer

EARTH'S TILT TODAY

N

N

Northern autumn

N

Northern
winter

N

Northern
autumn

N

Northern
summer

EARTH'S TILT IN
13,000 YEARS

N

N

Northern
winter

Northern
spring

Shorter summers and longer winters in the
northern hemisphere will have a big impact on
the Earth as a whole.

This is because most of Earth's land is in the
northern hemisphere, and land climates show
much more seasonal contrast than sea climates.

With changes to the strengths and lengths of
summers and winters in the north, there is potential
for new and bigger glaciers to form across large areas of
land above the equator.

LEO

CANCER

GEMINI

Experts today agree there are 88 constellations that help us to map out the night sky.

They include well-known examples such as Orion (the Hunter), Leo (the Lion), Taurus (the Bull), Cassiopeia (the Queen) and Sagittarius (the Centaur).

Throughout our lives we will be able to spot these and all the other constellations. However, these shapes won't last forever.

NEW CONSTELLATIONS
IN THE SKY

O n dark, clear nights, away from city lights, your eyes can pick out almost 2,000 stars in the sky. Looking at these stars you can imagine lines connecting groups of them to make patterns or shapes.

That's exactly what people of almost every culture have done throughout human history. They gave names to the shapes they imagined and told wonderful stories, legends and myths about them. Today we can see the same star patterns in the night sky – or constellations – that people in ancient cultures saw.

TAURUS

Bellatrix

Betelgeuse

ORION

Rigel

Saiph

CANIS
MAJOR

Not really grouped

The stars in a constellation can look close together because we are viewing them all from so very far away. It is important to remember that stars that have been 'linked' together in a constellation are not actually alongside one another in space. They are all at different distances from Earth.

Betelgeuse   Bellatrix   Earth

550–650 light years

In Orion, for example, the bright reddish star Betelgeuse is about 550–650 light years from Earth. It marks one shoulder of Orion the hunter. Bellatrix, which is on the hunter's other shoulder, is two or three times closer to us than Betelgeuse.

If there was a civilisation located in a different part of our galaxy, they would see a completely different arrangement of stars in their sky.

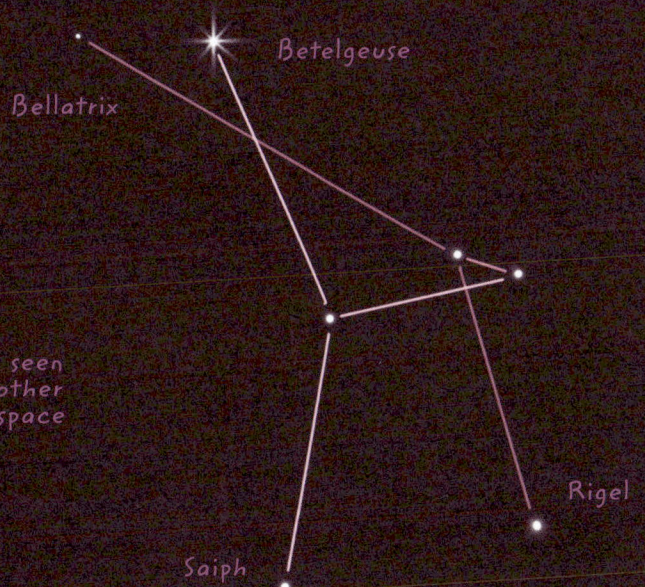

Betelgeuse

Bellatrix

*Orion as seen
from another
point in space*

Rigel

Saiph

19

Stars on the move

The reason our constellations' patterns will change is that the stars are also moving at different speeds. The stars are moving and jostling under gravitational forces as they travel in enormous orbits around the centre of our galaxy. Astronomers make careful measurements of how fast they are moving, and in what direction.

1 00,000 years from now, many constellations will no longer appear anything like they do today.

Stars can move at remarkable speeds of more than 10,000 km per hour, but because they are so far away it takes a long time for the movement to be noticeable to us on Earth. You can observe this idea in everyday life on a smaller scale. You can easily watch a car move from one end of the road to another just in front of you, but a distant jet aeroplane in the sky will seem to move much slower, even though it's actually zooming through the air at hundreds of kilometres an hour.

New legends and myths needed!

The Plough (or Big Dipper) is a famous part of the constellation Ursa Major (or Great Bear). Alkaid is the name of the star at the tip of the Plough, and it is moving in an entirely different direction to all the other stars that make up this shape today. In the distant future, the handle of the Plough will seem bent and the rest of the shape will be very spread out. It is going to look more like a duck than a plough!

THE PLOUGH

+ 100,000 years

ORION

The motion of Orion's stars 100,000 years in the future will make it look as though the hunter has lost his head!

LEO

THE CROSS

+ 100,000 years

The well recognised Southern Cross, or Crux constellation, in the southern hemisphere will appear as two parallel lines rather than a cross. Over this time the stars that make up Leo will have shifted to completely bend the back of the poor lion. Hopefully humans on our planet at that time will imagine the lion transformed into a fantastic new beast. Perhaps a cobra coiled up and ready to strike!

THE EXPLOSION OF
BETELGEUSE

Like everything else in nature, stars don't last forever. They are born, live and die over a life cycle that lasts billions of years. This is known as the evolution of a star.

Great balancing act

Stars are massive balls of hot gas held together by the force of gravity. Throughout its life a star faces a battle against this gravitational force, which is acting to try and make the star collapse in on itself. The fight back against this squeeze comes from the very hot centre, or core, of the star. Here, with gas tightly compacted and held at a temperature of more than **10 million °C**, we find the engine of the star.

In this central power station, reactions called fusion reactions between atoms produce enormous amounts of energy, called nuclear energy. This energy matches the pull of gravity trying to collapse the star. This keeps the star in balance, alive and stable. The battle between gravity pulling inwards and energy from the fusion reactions pushing outwards fuels all the billions of stars in our galaxy and keeps them shining for a very long time. But they can't shine forever.

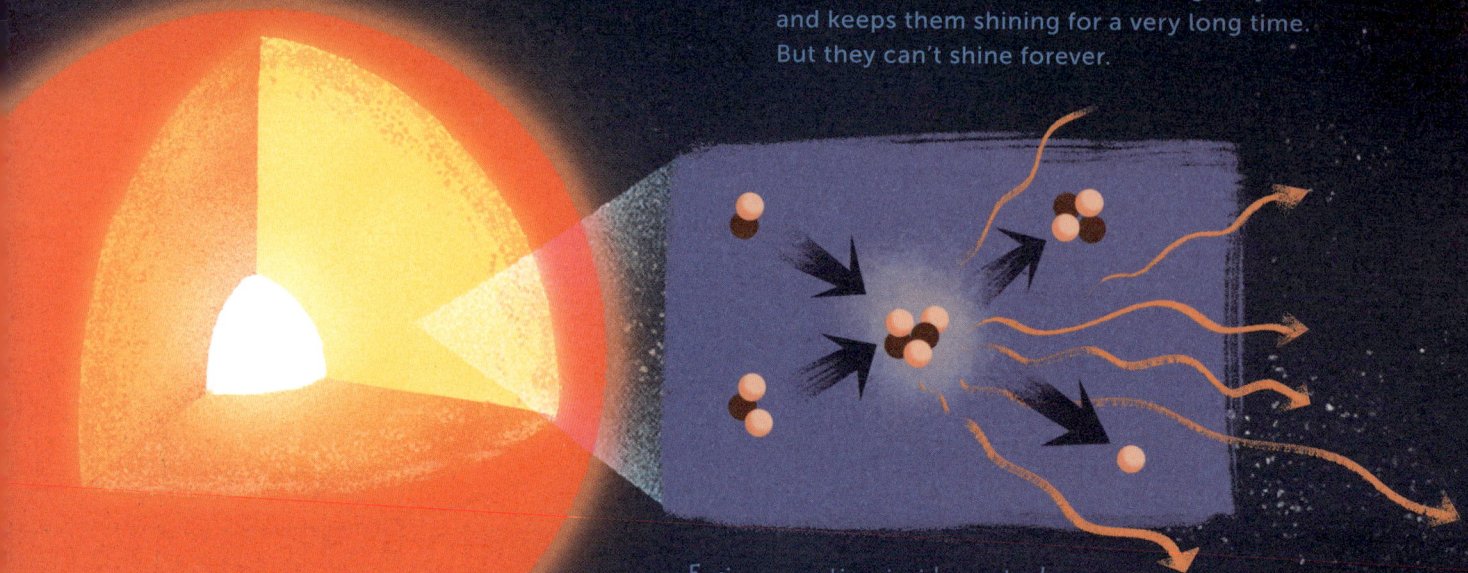

Fusion reaction inside a star's core

Over billions of years, a star uses up all its usable reaction fuel and runs out of energy. When this happens, gravity finally wins the battle and the death of the star begins.

Some stars go out with a bang!

The life cycle of each star – the time from its birth to death – is not the same. It depends on what mass a star had when it was first formed. The more mass a star has at birth, the quicker its life cycle, and the more explosive and violent its death.

Some massive stars are born with a mass that is up to a hundred times greater than that of our Sun! The most massive ones are only in balance and stable for a few million years. When their main hydrogen fuel source runs out, they first swell up into gigantic supergiant stars, using up their last bits of fuel. Then finally they are destroyed in an incredibly powerful explosion known as a supernova. A single supernova can briefly give out more light than an entire galaxy made of billions of stars!

Betelgeuse is unstable

The life of one well-known star in our sky is due to end within the next 1 million years of our future timeline. We've talked about the right shoulder of Orion the hunter, marked by one of the brightest stars we can see in the night sky, called Betelgeuse or alpha Orionis (see page 19). It is a dying, bloated supergiant star.

The star probably has a mass **20 times that of the Sun** and is estimated to be up to 1,000 times wider, too. If you swapped Betelgeuse for the Sun at the centre of our solar system, it would engulf all the planets up to Mars and the asteroid belt, too, filling up the solar system almost out to Jupiter!

Orion

Daytime supernova

Astronomers have been studying Betelgeuse closely for many years, using powerful telescopes to watch how its light is changing. Using their knowledge about the life cycle of stars, they have used computers to model (or predict) that Betelgeuse will explode into a supernova within the next million years.

When Betelgeuse blows up, humans on Earth will see it as a very bright beacon of light in the sky. Its light will be at least as bright as the full moon and even cast shadows at night. It will be a spectacular sight in the sky. For two to three months the supernova would even be seen in daytime! Thankfully, Betelgeuse is too far away for the explosion to harm life on Earth.

Strange leftovers

The supernova will throw out all the outer layers of gas and dust of the huge star and spread them into interstellar space. These leftovers of Betelgeuse will remain very hot for many years. Eventually they will drift across vast distances in space and be used as raw material for making a new generation of stars. It will be almost like a cosmic recycling plant!

Astronomers predict that, after the explosion has propelled away all the outer layers of Betelgeuse, the object left behind will be a strange, tightly squeezed star known as a neutron star (because they are made up of tiny particles called neutrons). These rapidly spinning stars are barely 20 km across.

A BUMP WITH THE
SOLAR SYSTEM

The stars you see with your eyes in the night sky are all inside our own Milky Way Galaxy. You've already learned that these stars, including the Sun, are continually moving. They all move in almost-circle-shaped orbits around the centre of our galaxy, which is so enormous that it takes 230 million years for the Sun to complete just one lap around it.

Sun position

Interestingly, the stars don't always stay quiet and orderly as they orbit the Milky Way. The billions of stars are jiggling in position due to the gravitational tugs between them. This means that as stars move around our galaxy, their wiggly paths can sometimes make them pass closer to one another.

Here comes Gliese 710

In December 2013 the European Space Agency (ESA) launched a telescope into space called Gaia. It was designed to measure the motion of millions of stars in our galaxy. One such star is called Gliese 710. This star is about half as wide as the Sun and lies almost 64 light years away towards the constellation of Serpens.

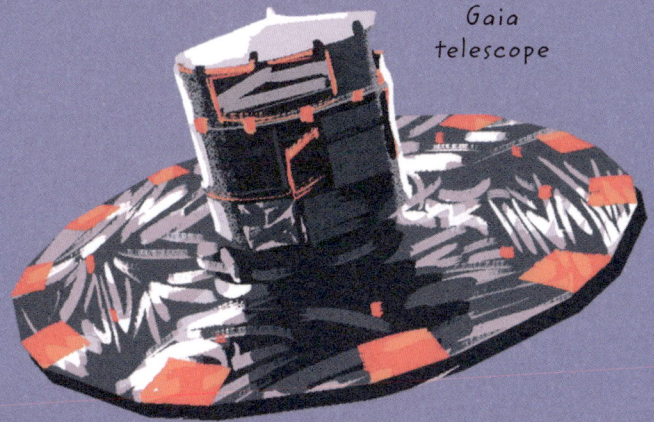

Gaia telescope

Our solar system

Gliese 710 is heading in our direction at a speed of about 50,000 km per hour. About 1.3 million years from now this rogue star will be a new visitor that bumps into our solar system! At its closest point to Earth, it will be seen as a brilliant orange object in the night sky that will outshine every other star on view.

The 150-million-km average distance between the Earth and Sun can be used as a unit of distance in space. It is called an Astronomical Unit (or AU). So, the Earth and Sun are 1 AU apart.

Astronomers have calculated that Gliese 710 will graze past our solar system about 13,300 AUs away. While this may seem very far away, by astronomical measures it is very close indeed for a star!

Gliese 710 heading towards us, many, many years from now

Shower of comets

Our bump with Gliese will cause some other
bumps as well! Far beyond all the planets in our
solar system, there is an enormous cloud of icy
material and rock from where most comets emerge.
This ball-shaped home to trillions of frozen comets
is known as the Oort cloud. It is named after the
Dutch astronomer Jan Oort, who first predicted
that comets come from this great outpost of
the solar system.

The Oort cloud is
thought to stretch from
around 2,000 AU to 100,000 AU
from the Sun. When Gliese 710 comes
closest to us 1.3 million years from now, it will
bump into the Oort cloud before gliding away.
The gravity of Gliese 710 will shake up a swarm
of icy rocks that reside there.

By disturbing the Oort cloud, Gliese 710 will send a shower of new comets towards the planets and Sun. Astronomers think we will get about 10 new comets per year flung into the inner solar system, and this comet parade may last a few million years! Some of the comets will be swept up by Jupiter's gravity, while others will circle the Sun in repeated orbits. A few may even be flung entirely out of the solar system.

MARS GETS A RING

The eight planets in our solar system can be grouped into two main types based on their size and what they are made of.

There are four rocky (or terrestrial) planets: Mercury, Venus, Earth and Mars. They orbit the Sun in the inner part of the solar system.

· Mercury

Venus

Earth

Mars

Jupiter

Well beyond Mars lie Jupiter, Saturn, Uranus and Neptune, which are giant gas planets.

The biggest planet, Jupiter, is more than 10 times the Earth's diameter.

Saturn

Uranus

Neptune

The smallest planet, Mercury, is 2.5 times smaller than Earth. You would need nearly 24,500 Mercurys to fill the volume of Jupiter!

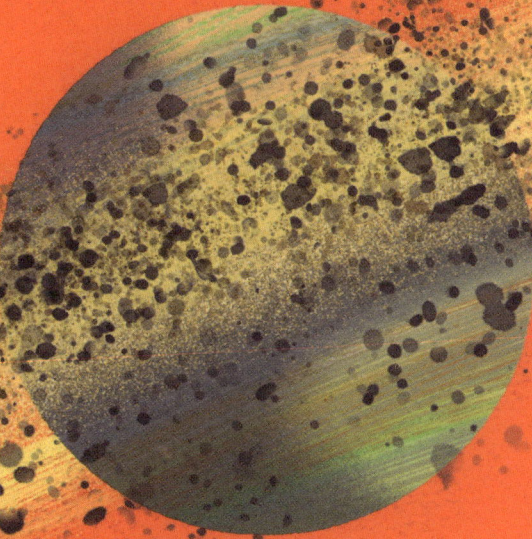

Saturn

Rings around the giants

The giant gas planets all have rings circling around them, but their ring systems are not all the same. Saturn has the brightest and most spectacular rings, made up of icy material that ranges in size from specks smaller than dust to boulders the size of a house.

Jupiter's rings are much fainter and made of tiny dark dust particles.

Jupiter

The rings of Uranus and Neptune are also very faint, and each ring is just a few kilometres wide, though some extend 100 km and up to 4,000 km at most.

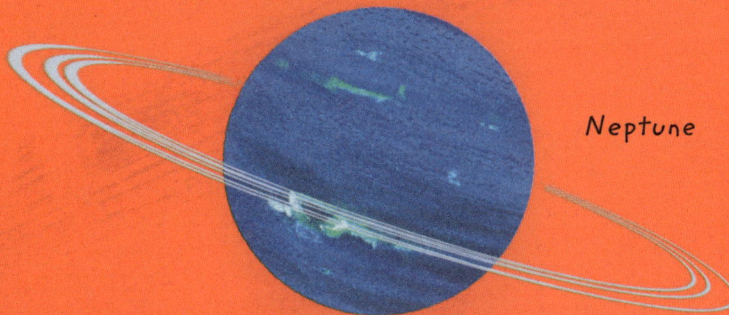

Neptune

Uranus

Astronomers believe that rings, such as those around Saturn, were made from the leftovers of moons that have been shattered into lots of small pieces of rock and ice. And there's about to be a new set of rings in the night sky. A tiny moon around Mars is facing a harsh fate along our future timeline of the Universe.

Doomed moon Phobos

Mars has two tiny moons called Phobos and Deimos. With strange potato-like shapes, the larger moon Phobos is just 22 km across, while Deimos is only 13 km wide. These two moons are among the smallest in the solar system.

Even from the surface of Mars, Phobos and Deimos look more like distant stars in the sky than moons. Spacecraft flown close to the moons have shown their surfaces are lumpy, with lots of craters and loose rocks.

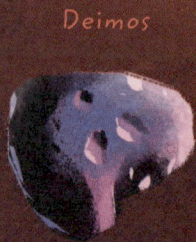

Deimos

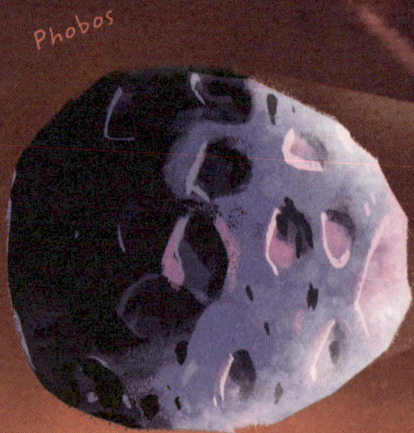

Phobos

Phobos is orbiting Mars at an average distance of only about 9,300 km. It zooms around the planet three times every Martian day. The fate of Phobos is a doomed one, however, and this moon won't spin around its planet forever. Phobos is slowly spiralling in towards Mars at a rate of 1.8 m every century.

Torn apart by gravity

As Phobos gets closer to Mars it will face stronger and stronger tugs from the planet's gravity. Since Phobos has an irregular, lumpy shape, the tugs that it feels from Mars' gravity are different on different parts of the little moon. Eventually, about 50 million years from now, the forces will become so strong that they will tear Phobos apart and smash it into smaller pieces.

The rubble, rocks and dust from the smashed moon will go into orbit around Mars. As this debris spreads out, Mars will become the first rocky planet in the solar system to have a ring! It will be a very dark and faint ring, much like Jupiter's ring.

The ring around Mars won't last too long though. Astronomers estimate it will have a lifetime of less than 100 million years. Slowly, the rubble that makes up the ring will crash onto the surface of Mars, leaving lots of new craters along the equator of the red planet.

In fact, the spacecraft sent near Phobos has beamed back pictures that show the moon is already starting to crack under the pressure of gravity. These early signs of a slow crumble are seen as long grooves along its surface today.

THE END OF
SOLAR ECLIPSES

A total eclipse of the Sun is one of the most beautiful sights in nature. The wondrous event happens when the Moon moves between the Earth and the Sun. If the three bodies are perfectly lined up, the Moon completely blocks out the bright light from the Sun and a shadow of the Moon is cast on Earth.

Those lucky enough to be located in the shadow see the spectacular sight of a total solar eclipse. For about 2–3 minutes, the day sky looks as dark as night and you can even see other stars! After this very brief time, the Moon glides away to once more reveal the full glare of the Sun, and the display is over.

Total solar eclipses are rare events. Though they are seen somewhere on Earth once every 18 months or so, most people only ever get to see them once in a lifetime. It can take between 360 and 400 years for a total solar eclipse to happen again in exactly the same location on Earth, such as your own town or city.

A stroke of luck!

The Sun is actually roughly 400 times larger in diameter than the Moon. It's amazingly lucky, then, that when seen from Earth, both objects appear to be about the same size. This happens because although the Sun is 400 times larger, it is also roughly 400 times further away from us than the Moon. If the Moon was slightly bigger or orbited a bit closer to Earth, the eclipses would not be as magnificent as they are today.

The Moon is drifting

During the Apollo missions to the Moon in the 1960s and 70s, astronauts placed mirrors on the Moon's surface, which are used to reflect beams of laser light from Earth. By measuring the time it takes the laser beam to travel from the Earth to the mirrors on the Moon and back, scientists can work out the distance to the Moon accurately. It turns out that the Moon is actually moving away from us at a rate of 3.8 cm per year!

Gravitational pull

High tide

This slow drift relates to the gravitational pull of the Moon on Earth. The Moon's gravity is tugging the oceans of our planet, making the tides rise. The Moon's pull on the oceans makes the Earth spin a tiny bit slower every day. At the same time, the oceans' pull on the Moon give it an energy boost, and it gets flung out to a higher orbit. So the Moon ends up moving very slowly further away from us.

The end of the eclipse show

As the Moon gently slips away from Earth, it will appear smaller in the sky as viewed by us on Earth. This means there will come a time in the distant future when the Moon will become too small in the sky to block out the whole of the Sun.

Astronomers have calculated the end of nature's great shadow show will begin about 600 million years in the future. In about 1.2 billion years, even partial eclipses of the Sun will be over. This will be when the Moon is too far from the Earth to ever cast any kind of shadow on our planet's surface.

In the distant future (many billions of years from now), the Earth's spin will have slowed so much that a day will be over 1,000 hours long, and the Moon will only be visible from one side of the Earth.

THE
GREAT ANDROMEDA
COLLISION

A galaxy is an enormous collection of stars, gas, dust and a mysterious substance known as dark matter, all held together by the force of gravity. In our own Milky Way Galaxy, the Sun is just one of about 250 billion stars that spin around the centre. At the very centre of our galaxy is an incredible supermassive black hole that has a mass of nearly 4 million Suns!

Grouped together

Galaxies rarely exist alone in space, and most often they are part of a group or cluster. Our Milky Way Galaxy is one of about 50 galaxies that make up a collection known as the Local Group. The galaxies in this group are spread over a region that is almost 10 million light years across. They are tied to each other by their gravitational forces, tugging them in different directions. Two massive spiral-shaped galaxies, our Milky Way and the Andromeda Galaxy, dominate the Local Group.

There are trillions of other galaxies in the Universe, some similar to ours and some very different.

Our giant neighbour

The Andromeda Galaxy is about 2.5 million light years from us, appearing in the constellation of Andromeda in the night sky. With a diameter of 220,000 light years, it is almost double the width of our galaxy. However, astronomers estimate that, despite the size difference, the two galaxies have more or less the same mass, which is about a trillion times that of the Sun.

The Andromeda Galaxy has an even more massive black hole at its centre, though, with a mass equal to more than 30 million Suns.

Heading our way

Using powerful telescopes such as the Hubble Space Telescope and the Gaia space observatory, astronomers have been carefully measuring the stars in the Andromeda Galaxy. Their studies show that it and the Milky Way Galaxy are heading towards one another.

The enormous gravitational pull of these massive galaxies is making them move together at a speed of about 402,000 km per hour. They will speed up further as they draw closer to one another.

Glancing blow

In about 4.5 billion years, the Andromeda Galaxy will finally crash with our galaxy. It is likely to be a cosmic brush-past rather than a full head-on collision. After the first crash, the galaxies will keep on looping around and pulling each other, locked in a gravitational dance. On each pass, stars will be thrown into long trails, like streamers in space.

A couple of billion years after the first glancing blow, Andromeda and the Milky Way will have fully merged into a single new enormous galaxy. With the two original central black holes merging, the mega galaxy will have an even greater supermassive black hole at its centre.

This great collision may throw our Sun and solar system farther out from the centre of the galaxy than we are today. There is no real danger of the Sun being destroyed, however.

When galaxies smash into each other, the stars inside them are spaced very far apart and rarely collide.

A sight to behold!

The coming together of Andromeda and the Milky Way will present a spectacular new sight in the night sky on Earth. About 2–3 billion years from now, the approaching Andromeda Galaxy will be a huge object in the sky, with its beautiful spiral shape clearly on view.

Another billion years or so later, the night sky will be lit up by an enormous number of new stars forming as the collision takes hold. When the two galaxies are fully merged, the central core of the new galaxy will be a vast, bright object to marvel at.

FUTURE CLOCK

A RED GIANT SUN

We saw on page 22 that the massive star Betelgeuse will end its life in a powerful supernova explosion. Our star, the Sun, has a lot less mass than Betelgeuse; we can even think of the Sun as a lightweight star. Like all other lightweight stars in the sky, the Sun's life cycle will end in a much less violent way.

For the past 4.6 billion years the Sun has been in balance. The energy from its fusion reactions keeps the Sun shining and warms the solar system. However, like Betelgeuse and all other stars, the matter the Sun consumes in its core will not last forever.

Big and bloated

The Sun is about halfway through its nuclear fuel. About 5 billion years in the future, the fuel will run out. The force of gravity will then take over and start to compress the ageing star. This squeezing of all the gas will make the centre of the Sun get even hotter.

The extra energy from this heat will then spread back outwards, which will make the upper layers of the Sun bloat and expand like a balloon. Sun-like stars at this stage of their life cycle can reach sizes of 100 million to 1 billion km in diameter. (In comparison, the Sun's diameter today is just 1.4 million km.)

As the energy of the Sun will then be spread over a much larger area, its temperature will become cooler, reaching only around 3,000°C at the surface. That is about half as hot as it is today.

The lower temperature will make the Sun shine red, transforming it into what's called a red giant.

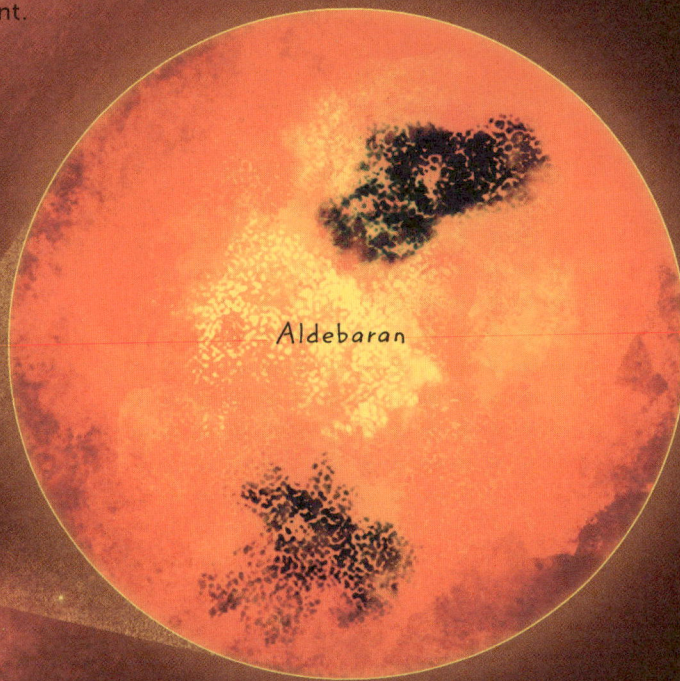

Aldebaran

On a clear night, you can look out for bright red giant stars using just your eyes. These stars are older than the Sun and have gone further along in their life cycles.

Giants in the sky

Aldebaran is the reddish star in the constellation of Taurus (the Bull). It is 65 light years away and has a radius 40 times that of the Sun today. Another example is Arcturus, the brightest star in the constellation of Bootes (the Herdsman). It has a radius 25 times that of the Sun and puts out more than 100 times the total light of the Sun.

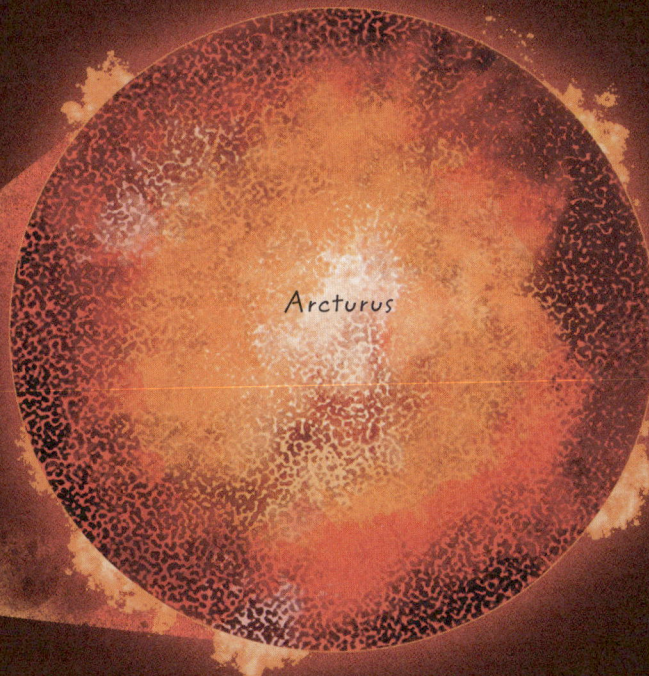

Arcturus

Scorched Earth

When, more than 5 billion years from now, the Sun swells into a red giant star, it will swallow up the two closest planets, Mercury and Venus.

Astronomers have calculated that, at its largest, the radius of the Sun may be 250 times bigger than it is today. In this case, even the Earth will be gobbled up.

If the Earth enters the Sun's atmosphere, it will be broken up by the hot gas particles and spiral further inwards.

Earth

Red giant Sun

There is, however, a chance that the Earth's orbit around the Sun will move outwards slightly before the red giant Sun can engulf it. If the Earth does escape its grasp, it would still be so close that the incredible heat would scorch our planet. The oceans would boil off, the atmosphere would be stripped away and it would be impossible for life to survive. Earth would be left as a sizzling, molten ball.

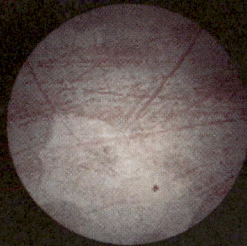

Europa

JUPITER

A new home?

The good news is that as the red giant Sun expands across the inner solar system, its heat will warm up some of the objects that are today frozen in the outer parts of the solar system. Europa, the small moon of Jupiter, and Enceladus, the icy moon of Saturn, have vast amounts of slushy ice beneath their surfaces today.

The extra heat from the Sun could turn these into huge liquid oceans, making them possible new homes for humans of the future. Although the heat could also turn them into complete water-worlds as well!

Further out, the dwarf planet Pluto might have surface temperatures close to the average temperature on Earth today, making it another place humans might live.

THE DEATH OF THE SUN

After the Sun has turned into a red giant star, it will enter the final stages of its billions-of-years-long life cycle. The red giant phase will last about 1/10th of its full lifetime, then the Sun will enter a new stage where it will not be stable, with many shudders and changes in the light it puts out.

Cocooned in bubbles

Over the next few billion years, the outer layers of the Sun will completely separate and float away from the central part that contains the tightly packed core. The ejected layers of gas will glow in a range of colours, using the energy of the hot core that is left behind.

The shrugged off layers of gas make a beautiful object called a planetary nebula. The name is a bit confusing because there are no planets in these nebulae, but they got their name because they *look* a bit like planets when viewed using small telescopes.

Right now in the night sky, you can see many examples of stars that have already reached this phase of their life cycle. Two fantastic examples are the Cat's Eye Nebula, within the constellation of Draco, and the Butterfly Nebula, in the constellation of Scorpius. These are spectacular objects in space, with stunning shapes and colours on display.

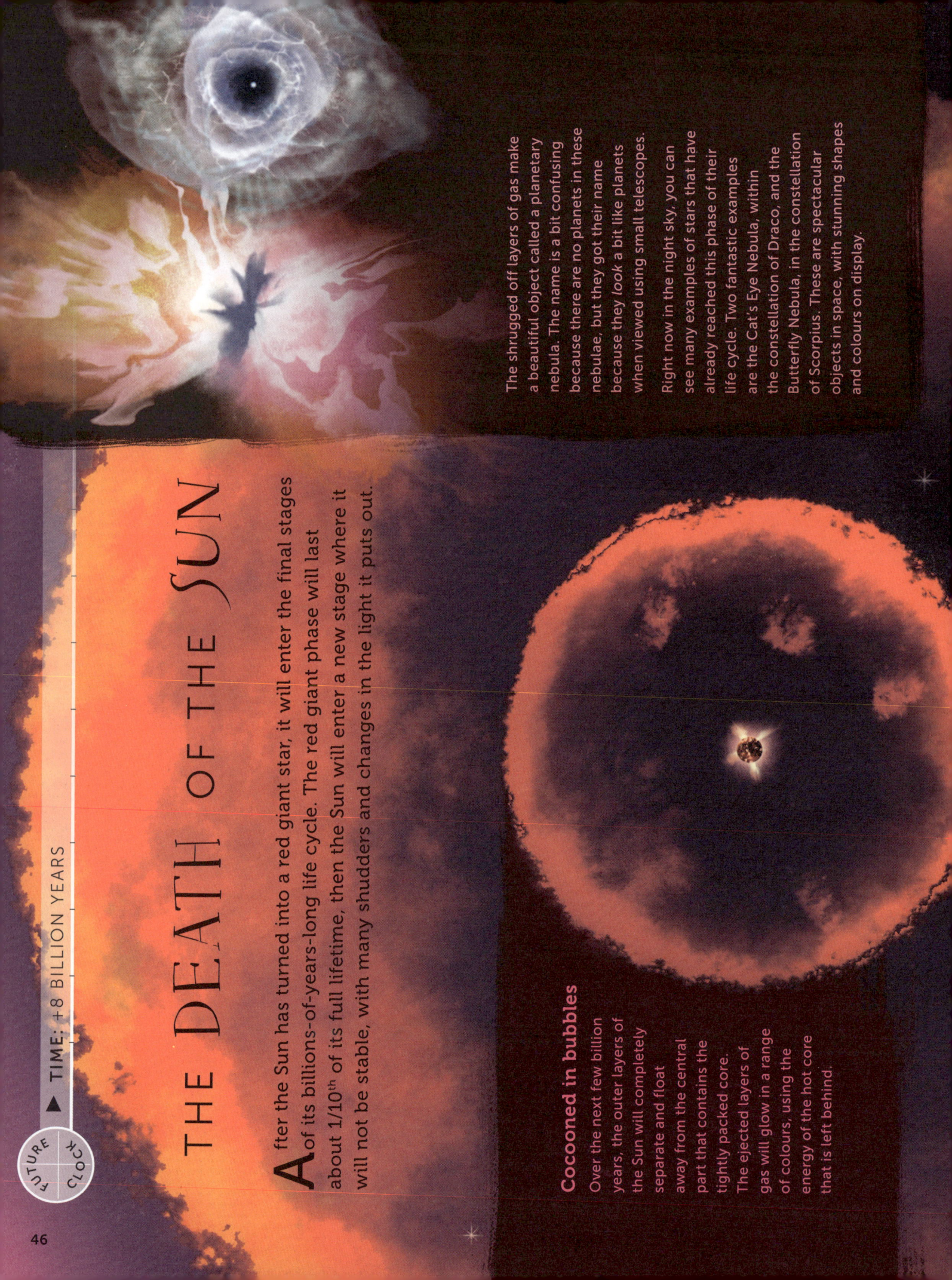

Crushed leftover

Next, the remaining outermost layers of our Sun will peel off into space. About 8 billion years from today, all that's left behind will be its bare core, squeezed tightly by the force of gravity surrounded by the planetary nebula. Made mostly of carbon and oxygen, this leftover Sun will only be about the size of the Earth today.

In this form it will be a very strange object known as a white dwarf star. Inside a white dwarf star, the matter is so tightly packed that if you brought a teaspoon of its material to Earth, it would weigh more than an elephant!

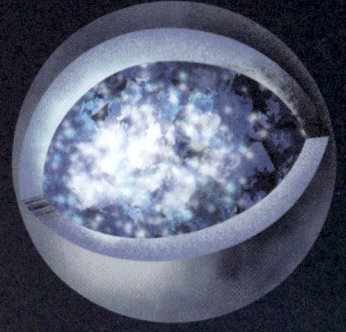

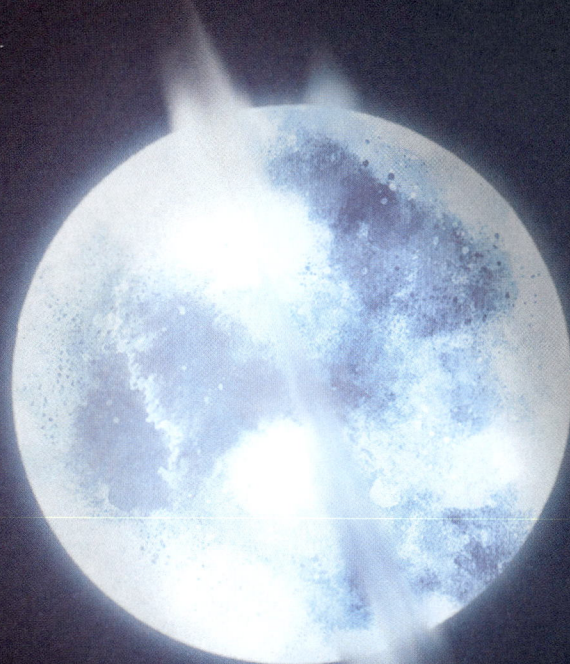

Diamonds in the sky

The heat from the white dwarf Sun will slowly fade away. Like a piece of coal out of the fire, over millions of years it will fizzle out and dim forever. As it turns into a dark, cold object, the carbon and oxygen particles that it is made of will begin to freeze and form crystals. Cold carbon can crystallise to form diamond. So, our Sun may well end its life as an Earth-sized diamond in the sky!

GATHERING OF GALAXIES

When we think of the whole Universe, we picture it loaded with galaxies. Astronomers estimate there may be between 100 billion and 2 trillion galaxies in the Universe, each packed with billions of stars. These many galaxies are millions to billions of light years away from us.

Astronomers are using large, powerful telescopes to map out the locations of many millions of them, making a master plan of the Universe. Their measurements show that most of the galaxies are organised into groups and clusters, with the force of gravity acting as the glue holding them loosely together.

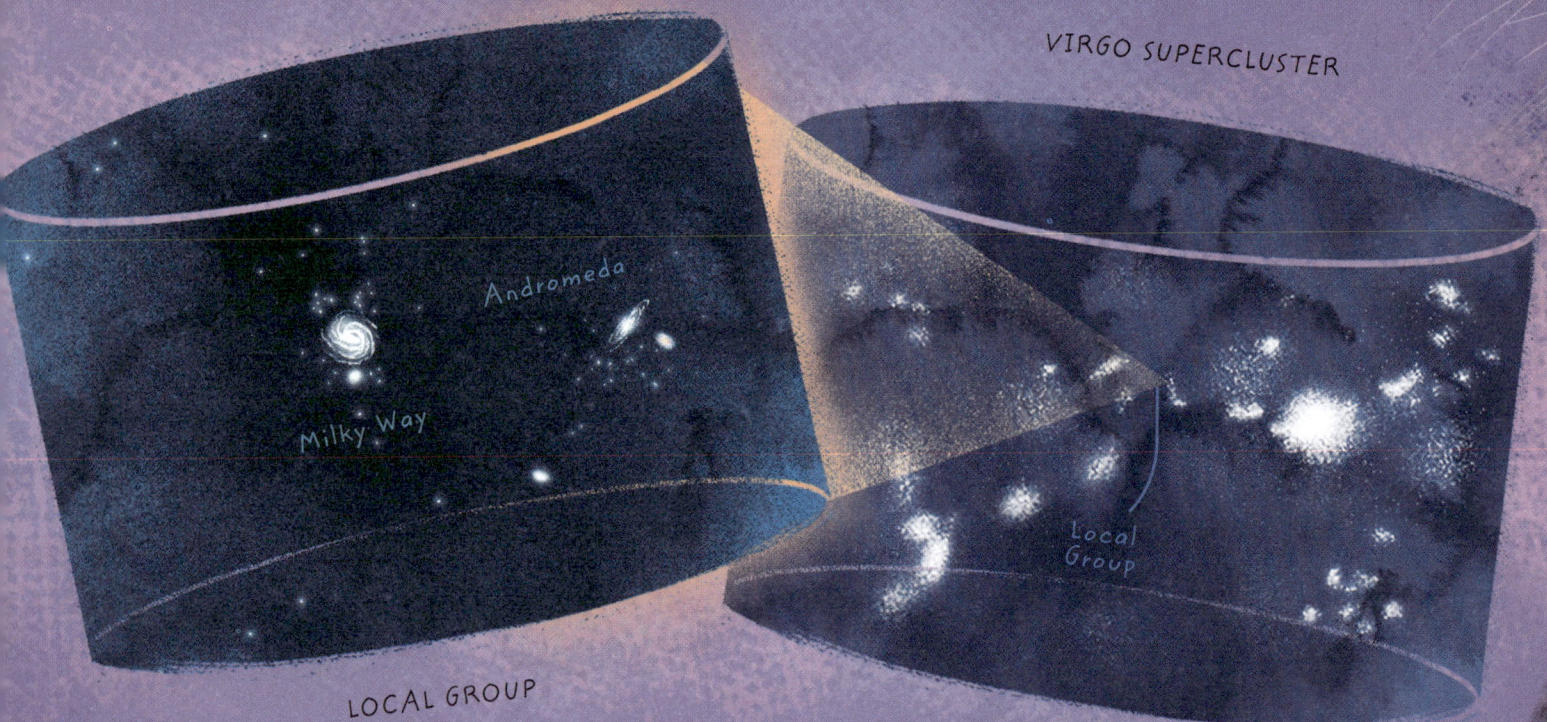

VIRGO SUPERCLUSTER

Andromeda

Milky Way

Local Group

LOCAL GROUP

Grandest structures in space

We saw on page 38 that our Milky Way Galaxy is part of a Local Group of about 50 galaxies, including the magnificent Andromeda Galaxy. It turns out that collections of galaxies, such as the Local Group, are themselves surrounded by many other groups of galaxies, to form even larger structures. On an even larger scale, our Local Group and hundreds of other clusters of galaxies are clumped together into a super-sized collection known as the Virgo supercluster. This swarm of galaxies stretches across an area of space more than 100 million light years in diameter.

The Universe is so incredibly large, that even the Virgo supercluster is part of something bigger called Laniakea, which also includes other large superclusters. Laniakea is about 500 million light years across and contains 100 million billion times the mass of the Sun.

So, your full address in the Universe would be written as:

LANIAKEA

Virgo supercluster

Your house number, street, city, county, Earth, Solar system, Milky Way Galaxy, Local Group, Virgo supercluster, Laniakea!

You can picture the Universe as a web-like pattern of galaxies, forming enormous chains and walls that spread over billions of light years.

A coming together

The Virgo supercluster is built roughly like an almost-flat rugby ball. Sitting near the centre is a cluster of about 2,000 galaxies.

Other galaxy clusters are peppered about and the Local Group (including the Milky Way Galaxy) is closer to the edge of the Virgo supercluster. There is an enormous gravitational pull among the many galaxies, and over a very long period, matter in the clusters is being attracted closer and closer together.

Thanks to our understanding of the Universe, and by mapping out how the galaxies are moving, astronomers have measured that many of the galaxies around the superclusters' outer parts are falling inwards. They predict that about 100 billion years in the future, the Virgo supercluster will have pulled all its matter into a single enormous mass of stars.

The Great Attractor

So our supercluster set of galaxies are headed for one another, but there is also a curious mass in the Universe known as the Great Attractor. This mysterious region of the Universe has a collection of mass that equals tens of thousands of Milky Ways. Its gravity is so powerful that it is drawing in galaxies over a region hundreds of millions of light years across.

Our entire supercluster is also heading towards the Great Attractor. It is thought to be up to 250 million light years away, but we don't know what really lies there. Because the disk of our Milky Way Galaxy contains lots of gas, dust and stars, it muddies our view of that region, keeping it cloaked in mystery.

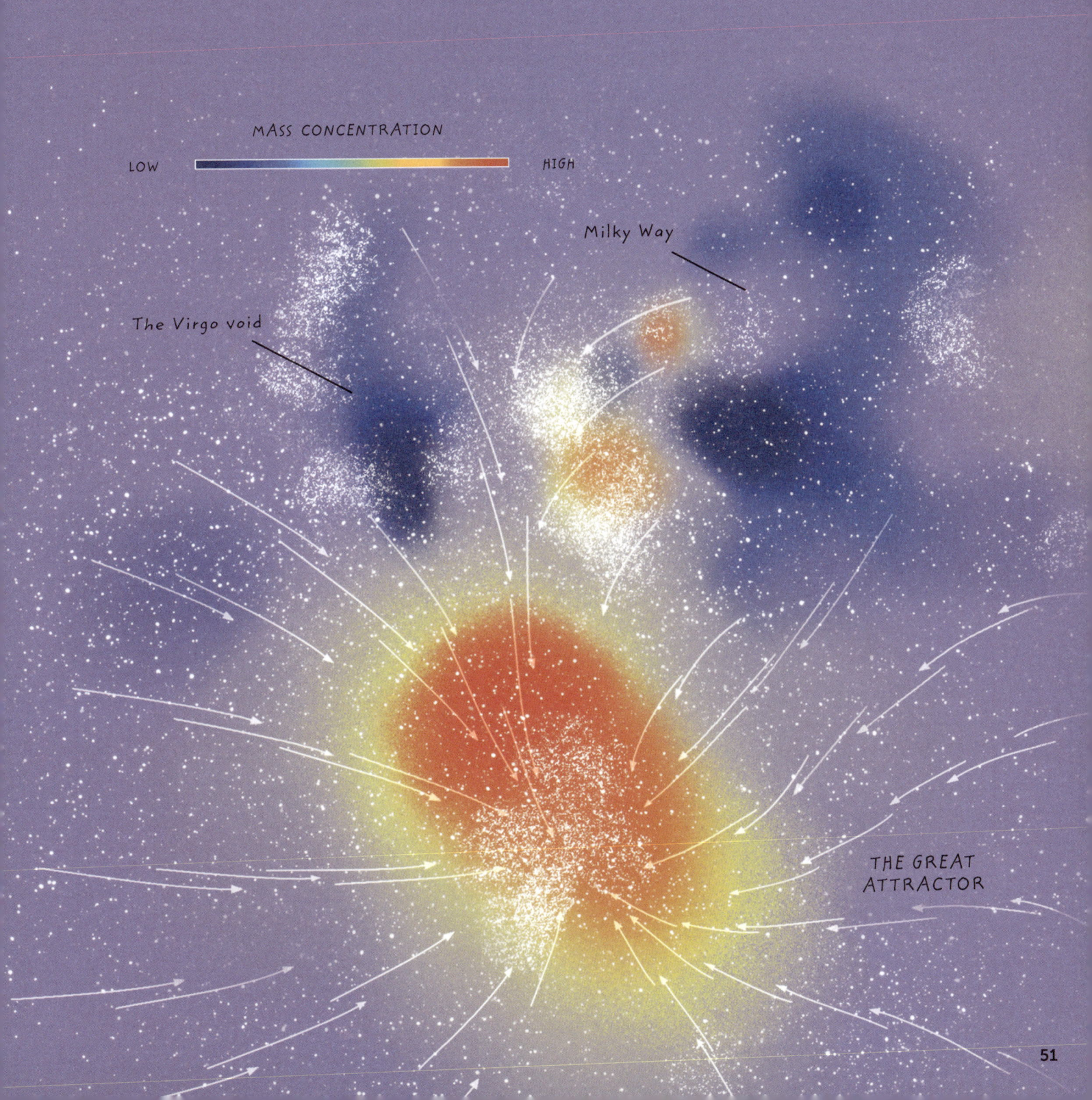

MASS CONCENTRATION

LOW HIGH

Milky Way

The Virgo void

THE GREAT ATTRACTOR

DISAPPEARING UNIVERSE

The Universe has not always been the same size. It has been growing ever since it began 13.8 billion years ago. Scientists call it the expanding Universe. The area of space we see today is billions of times bigger than it was when the Universe was very young. It is getting bigger right at this moment.

Galaxies going along for a ride

To help understand an expanding Universe, imagine it as a loaf of bread dough that has raisins in it. In this model, think of each raisin as a cluster or group of galaxies, such as the Virgo supercluster we saw earlier. As bread dough rises and expands, the raisins move further away from each other, though they are still all firmly in the dough.

Galaxies in our Universe sit in the space around them, as the raisins sit in the dough. As the space between the galaxies expands, it carries them further apart.

Big Bang

The galaxies are riding along in an expanding Universe.

Further and further away

On page 48 we came across galaxies gathering together under the force of gravity. This only happens on what astronomers think of as a small patch of the Universe. (Even though it may be 100 million light years across!) The Universe is so unimaginably enormous that the galaxy clusters in one part of it are all actually moving **away** from the galaxy clusters in another part, even as the galaxies within each cluster move towards each other.

It turns out that as we discover galaxies further away, the faster they seem to be moving away from us. As the Universe continues expanding over time, more and more galaxies are getting so far away that they leave our sight and their light will now never reach us.

A strange, dark energy is out there

In the early 20th century, scientists such as Albert Einstein, Georges Lemaître and Edwin Hubble showed that the Universe was expanding. Ever since, most scientists thought that the rate at which the Universe is expanding would get slower in the time since the Big Bang. They expected the gravity from all the billions of galaxies would pull back on space and slow the spread.

Amazingly, in the late 1990s, when astronomers measured how the Universe was changing, they discovered that it is actually expanding faster today than it did when it was much younger! The faster expansion of the Universe is a great mystery.

Scientists think there must be something in space that's acting against gravity and dark matter, pushing the Universe apart faster and faster. This mysterious part of the Universe has been named dark energy. No one really knows what exactly dark energy is, but there's a lot of it. Nearly 68 per cent of the Universe is made of dark energy!

Beyond the horizon

In the very far future, with the Universe incredibly stretched apart, our neighbourhood in space will slowly become much emptier than it is today. There will come a time, roughly 3 trillion years in the future, when nearly all galaxies are out of our reach, no matter how hard we look. They will be moving away from us quicker than their light has time to reach our eyes. The Universe of billions of galaxies we see today will have disappeared from view.

LAST STARS STANDING

We have seen earlier in this book that not all stars are the same. Looking out into space today we can see young and old stars, dwarf stars and enormous supergiants, lightweight and massive stars. Another difference among stars is their lifespan. They don't all live for the same amount of time.

Cosmic recycling

The stars are taking part in an incredible recycling scheme! When an old star dies, its outer layers are spewed out as a supernova explosion or puffed out as a planetary nebula. This gas is pushed out into space, where it glides huge distances until it reaches clouds of other gas and dust that are gathering to make new stars. These clouds in interstellar space are star-making factories, where the matter is squeezed in by gravity to start a new generation of stars.

Star-making is already coming to an end

The Universe is already past its glory days of making stars. By studying galaxies that have different ages, astronomers have worked out that we're surrounded by mostly old stars made during a 'boom time' between 11 and 9 billion years ago. Almost 90 per cent of the stars we see around us today were made during the past 10 billion years or so. Today, the rate at which new stars are being made in galaxies is less than 5 per cent of its peak rate during the boom.

The Universe is only likely to make about 5 per cent more stars than exist today. We are already seeing the beginning of the end of star-making factories. But the whole 'ending' will take trillions of years, so don't worry! This is thanks to the huge number of exceptionally long-lived stars populating our Universe.

Over trillions of years, this recycling of old star matter to make new stars will continue. There will come a time, though, when so many cycles like this will have been completed that all the raw material for making new stars will have been used up. It will all have been transformed, with much of it locked up in dead stars, such as white dwarfs, neutron stars and black holes.

Little red dwarfs

The most common type of star in the Universe is a red dwarf. In our Milky Way Galaxy alone between half and three-quarters of the stars are red dwarfs. These tiny stars have masses that can be a tenth of our Sun's and have a surface temperature of around 3,000°C (or about half that of the Sun).

We saw on page 23 that a star's lifespan depends on its mass when it was first formed. The more massive a star, the faster it uses up its fuel supply and the shorter its life. Since they have so little mass, red dwarf stars use up their nuclear fuel supply very slowly. They just don't have as much work to do to support themselves against gravity.

Because of this, these little red stars can last for 10 trillion years or more. They will be the last stars to die out. Their faint light will send out the final beams of starlight left in the Universe.

Red dwarf

Black dwarf

Eventually, like all stars, even red dwarfs will finally burn through their supply of fuel. When they do, all their heat will escape into space and they will turn into cold, essentially invisible black dwarf stars.

THE FINAL ACTS OF THE UNIVERSE

We end our incredible journey into the future by looking into the final fate of the Universe itself. We have seen that the Universe has been expanding ever since it started in a Big Bang. The expansion is speeding up as time passes by, due to that mysterious force called dark energy.

Heat death

The final acts of the Universe will be ruled over by its never-ending expansion. Galaxy clusters and single galaxies will get more and more isolated in space. Contact among galaxies will be lost. There'll be no light emerging from all the dead stars and dark black holes will be left wandering the Universe. In the very distant future, it's predicted that black holes themselves will evaporate from the Universe. Particles such as protons that make up all matter may also decay.

And at an unimaginably enormous time in the future, written as 1 followed by 30 zeros years, the only things left in the Universe will be a few very strange particles and hardly anything will put out any energy. The Universe will be left cold, dark and empty. This is known as the heat death of the Universe.

The Big Rip

Some scientists believe there may be a very dramatic finale for the Universe. If dark energy gets even more powerful in the future, then we could have quite an active destruction of the Universe.

The enormous and growing strength of dark energy would start to overwhelm everything. It would pull apart galaxies, stars, planets and anything else left at that point in the far-distant future. Even molecules and atoms could be shredded by the ever-faster expansion of space. The force of dark energy would be much greater than gravity and all other forces that hold objects together.

The Universe would end with a Big Rip – everything torn apart before vanishing from view.

Don't worry! If the prediction of a Big Rip is correct, it won't start for trillions and trillions of years in the future and who knows what human life and technology will look like at that point! To truly know how the Universe will end we will need to discover what dark energy really is. We do not yet know whether it will stay the same forever, become much stronger, or even just fade away.

Catch the wonders of the Universe today

The Universe is so incredible and fascinating because everything in it is continually changing. We know that our planet, the solar system, our Milky Way Galaxy, the local galaxy cluster and the entire Universe will not stay the same forever, but we also know it's truly beautiful right now. When you next look up at the wonders of the night sky, think of all the changes that are slowly taking place.

Stars, planets and moons are on the move. The Sun is ageing and some of the brightest stars in the sky today will become the supernovae of tomorrow. Our galaxy is drifting towards another huge spiral galaxy, but all the other very distant galaxies are racing away from each other. All this time, the space you are watching is getting larger and larger. The future of the Universe is unfolding before our eyes.

GLOSSARY

astronomer A scientist who studies the stars, planets, and other natural objects in space.

Astronomical Unit (AU) Used as a unit of distance in space, the 150-million-km average distance between the Earth and Sun is 1 AU.

atmosphere The envelope of gases surrounding the Earth or another planet.

axis An imaginary line that a planet rotates around.

black dwarf star The final stage at the death of a star, when the star's fuel has run out.

black hole A small region of space with such strong gravity that light cannot escape it.

comet Small body made of rock, dust and ice, which orbits the Sun.

constellation An area of the sky containing a pattern of stars that was invented by humans.

dark matter A mysterious material which exists in space, which could be randomly moving particles created after the Big Bang.

equator An imaginary line drawn around the middle of the Earth or other planet.

fundamental A key or important part of something.

fusion The reaction between atoms that produces enormous amounts of energy.

galaxy A large number of stars, gas, dust and dark matter, held together by gravity.

gravity A force that attracts all objects towards one another. The strength of the force depends on the objects' masses.

Great Attractor A huge mass in the Universe whose gravity is so powerful that it draws galaxies towards it.

hydrogen A colourless gas that is the lightest and most common element in the Universe.

light year The distance light travels in one year, a unit used to measure distances in astronomy.

Local Group A group of about 50 galaxies that includes the Milky Way.

orbit The path of one object around another in space, such as a planet around a star.

organism An animal, plant or other living thing.

particle A small piece of matter.

planetary nebula Formed when a star can no longer support itself by fusion reactions at its centre.

red dwarf A tiny star with a small mass, which means it will use up its fuel supply very slowly.

red giant An ageing star, with a slightly lower surface temperature that makes it shine red.

solar eclipse When the Moon passes directly in front of the Sun when viewed from Earth, and the Moon's shadow falls on Earth.

supercluster A group of galaxy clusters. The Local Group is part of the Virgo supercluster.

supergiant A massive, luminous star with a life cycle of probably only a few million years.

supernova An incredibly powerful explosion created when a star's fuel eventually runs out.

white dwarf The remains of a star once the outer layers have peeled away.

FIND OUT MORE

BOOKS FOR THE SKY EXPLORER

Wonders of the Night Sky
by Professor Raman Prinja

Inviting readers all over the world to look up – just as curious people before them have done for millennia – and to *know why* each wonder appears before their eyes. This beautiful book connects readers to the many parts of the Universe visible to the naked eye against the sky, explodes them on the page, then provides inspiring connections to the science behind the stellar backdrop.

9781526312181 – Wayland, 2022

International Space Station
by Clive Gifford

Written to inspire a new generation of astronauts, this detailed and fact-filled text will make you think you've visited the space station yourself.

9781526302175 – Wayland, 2018

A Guide to Space
by Kevin Pettman

An infographic-style guide to space – a bumper-book packed with facts and stats in vivid colour.

9781526307378 – Wayland, 2019

WEBSITES FOR THE SKY EXPLORER

Scale of the Universe:

scaleofuniverse.com

Here's your chance to explore and understand the vast size of the Universe. You can use a slide to move from Earth, across the solar system, and on to stars, galaxies and the whole Universe.

Earth and Moon viewer:

www.fourmilab.ch/earthview

From this website you can view Earth, the Moon and planets from different locations in the solar system. You can also view Venus, Mercury and Mars, plus some moons. You can pretend to be at the Moon and see what Earth looks like from there!

Space weather:

www.spaceweather.com

Go here for updated, daily information on activity occurring on the Sun's surface, such as sunspots and flares.

Tonight's sky:

hubblesite.org/resource-gallery/learning-resources/tonights-sky

A rolling series of videos telling you which constellations are on view each month.

The planets today:

www.theplanetstoday.com

Take a look at where all the planets are in their orbits around the Sun today. You can even run the clock forward to see how their positions change.

For taking your astronomy further:

www.rmg.co.uk/royal-observatory

Check out Royal Observatory Greenwich's 'Look Up!' podcast and *Night Sky Highlights* blog. Both are released monthly with exciting and clear guides to more amazing details about the Universe.

www.youtube.com/c/RoyalObservatoryGrnwich

And don't forget their 'Astronomy at Home' video playlist on YouTube for lots of engaging activities and other resources.

INDEX